FRANKLIN WATTS PICTURE ATLAS

Deserts
and Wastelands

Dougal Dixon

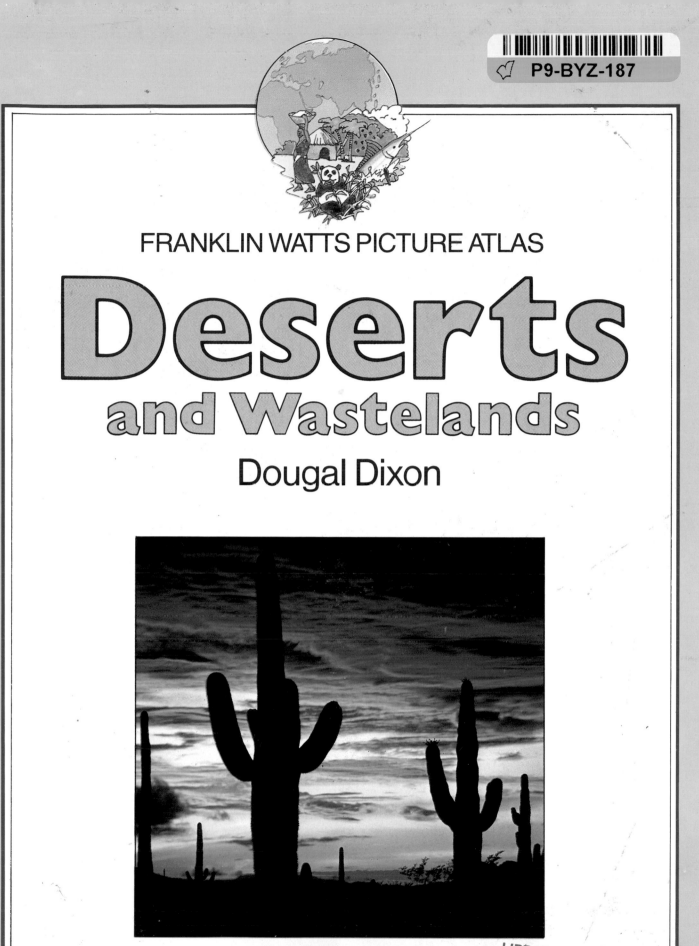

FRANKLIN WATTS
London · New York · Toronto · Sydney

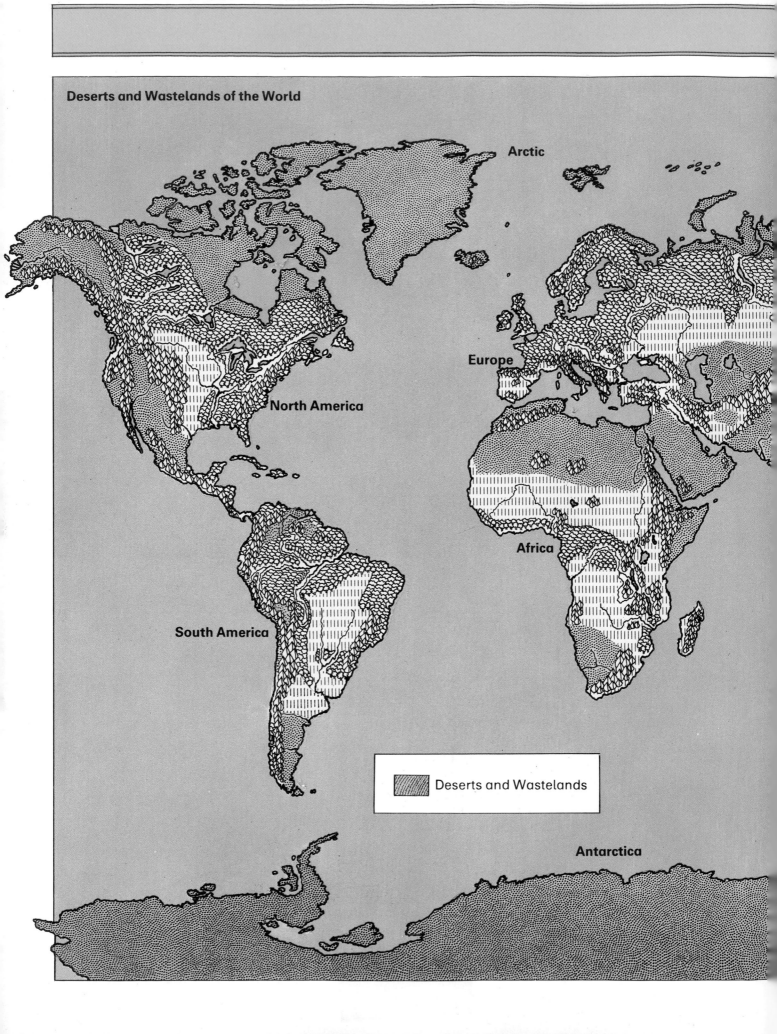

Deserts and Wastelands of the World

Arctic

Europe

North America

Africa

South America

Deserts and Wastelands

Antarctica

Foreword

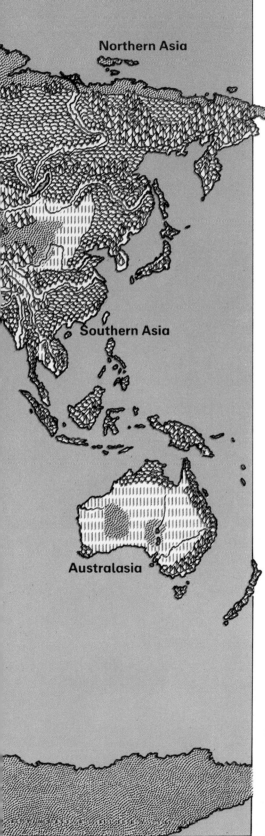

Northern Asia

Southern Asia

Australasia

Sand and heat – that is what a desert means to most of us. Waterless expanses stretch to the horizon in all directions, and not a sign of life anywhere. The Sun scorching down, shrivelling up any creature that dares to venture out into the merciless glare.

Yet the desert is not all like that. Sandy wastes only occupy a small proportion of the desert areas of the world – the rest consisting of rock, shattered stone or salt and clay. The days are, indeed, hot but the nights can be bitterly cold. The lowest temperatures are at the North and South Poles, which we must also regard as deserts because of their dryness and their hostility to life.

However, even under all these harsh conditions life manages to exist. The hottest, driest wastes have seeds waiting for a brief wet season in which to start growing, and deep in the sand small creatures lie, waiting for the cool evening when they can creep out to forage. Cold, bleak corners of the Antarctic continent may have lichens and tiny insects, evolved to withstand the lowest temperatures. People, too, have learnt to cope with the desert, although, despite the fact that deserts occupy over one fifth of the world's land surface, a mere five per cent of the world's population lives in them.

Contents

Deserts Hot and Cold

A desert is a region with very little water — we can actually define a desert as an area with less than 30cm (12in) of rain per year. This may sound quite a lot, and indeed it is in the desert, as it all falls at once within a few days. The remainder of the year can be, and usually is, totally dry.

The hot deserts mainly occur along two belts around the globe at about the latitudes of the Tropic of Cancer and the Tropic of Capricorn. The air rising at the Equator is hot and wet. But as it moves north and south it loses its moisture in tropical rain forests, to descend as hot dry air masses on the desert belts. On top of this there are three conditions that prevent rain from being brought in by local winds — and these three conditions give us three distinct types of desert.

Types of desert

Cool coastal deserts are found by the sea, where cold ocean currents bathe the edge of the land. The coldness of the water causes the air mass to descend, and as rain usually only falls where an air mass rises, the climate tends to be very dry. Further inland, away from the coast are rain shadow deserts and interior continental deserts. Any moisture that blows from the sea will have fallen as rain long before it reaches the latter, very remote places. Rain shadow deserts form on the sheltered sides of mountain chains; rain falling on the windward slopes as the air rises over the mountains, leaving dry air to waft onto the plains beyond.

The erosion of deserts by rain and wind causes some very strange-shaped

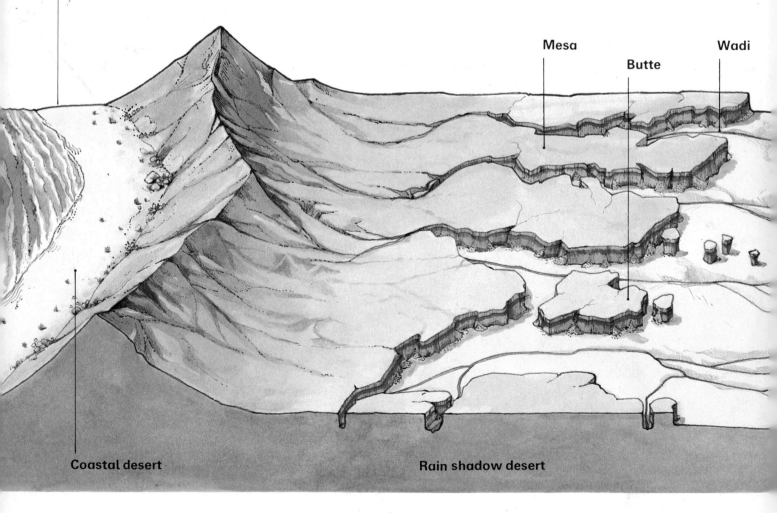

Mesa

Butte

Wadi

Coastal desert

Rain shadow desert

formations. Mesas, flat table-topped hills; buttes, peaks of hard rock left as the surrounding land is eroded down and wadis. Wadis are dry river beds in the sand. When flash floods occur, these dry wadis become raging torrents which run over the parched land. As the rain stops, and the wadi dries up, it forms an alluvial fan at the end of its course, from the deposits that it has carried with it.

Sand and the formations it creates, dunes of different types, are what people usually think of as a desert, with maybe the odd oasis dotting the otherwise dry waste. Oases occur where the underground rock is just below the surface and so any water in the sand collects, creating small patches of ground where vegetation can grow.

Cold deserts

The cold deserts of the North and South Poles are also arid wastelands because of the severe lack of rainfall. Water is usually in the form of ice and snow. Erosion in the tundra regions is mainly by ice, where the surface can thaw and refreeze with the passing of the seasons. This expansion and contraction causes the rocks to crack and split and, as a result, the ground is sometimes thrown up into shallow domes. Stones rolling off these domes gather in the hollows between them forming vast honeycomb patterns. Other, larger domes, called "pingos" sometimes rise to 100m (330ft). It is not certain how these form, but it is probably from underground streams rising up to freeze on the surface.

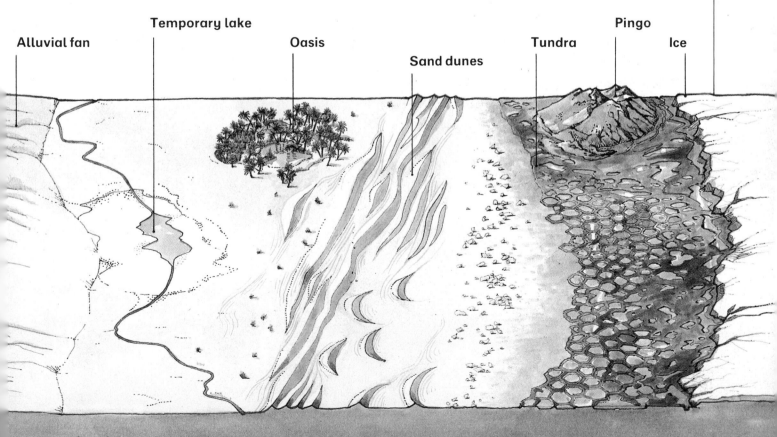

Alluvial fan   **Temporary lake**   **Oasis**   **Sand dunes**   **Tundra**   **Pingo**   **Ice**

Interior continental desert

Desert Landscapes

Wherever rocks are exposed, they break down and are washed away by natural processes. In temperate and humid areas this is mostly done through the process called weathering, in which chemicals dissolved in the rain react with those of the rock to break it up. In the desert there is hardly any rain and so there is little chemical breakdown of the rocks. Most erosion is through physical processes.

And in such harsh conditions, the physical processes can be very strong. The great range of temperature between day and night can expand and contract a rock, weakening it and splitting it open. The fierce wind shifts the finest stone fragments, blasting them against exposed rocks and grinding both fragments and rocks down into that commodity that seems so typical of deserts – sand.

Sand deserts

Sand starts as tiny crystals of quartz that break off granite rock. Eventually, these may compress to form sandstone, which is weathered and eroded in turn. The wind picks up these tiny particles and carries them along the ground. Dunes are caused by the wind. As the wind blows the sea of sand, it shapes it into big ridges or small ripples – like the surface of the ocean.

"Seif" dunes are long ridges of sand with bare rock between. They can be up to 40m (130ft) high, 600m (1960ft) wide and 400km (250 miles) long. The wind blows parallel to the dune, but it may vary its direction. "Barchan" dunes, on the other hand, occur in areas where the wind blows from a single direction. Barchans are isolated, crescent-shaped dunes that slowly move downwind, with their "horns" pointing forwards.

Other types of dunes are longitudinal and transverse dunes. The first occur when stronger one-way winds move both fine and heavier sand, cutting long troughs parallel with the path of the wind. Transverse dunes are the product of moderate one-way winds which move only fine, lighter sand grains. Tumbling wind eddies swirl the heavier grains, while lifting the lighter grains to create the ridges.

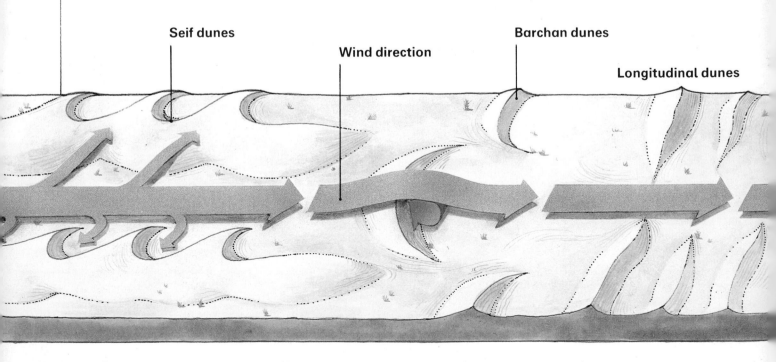

Seif dunes

Wind direction

Barchan dunes

Longitudinal dunes

Rock deserts

In actual fact, only 20 per cent of the world's deserts consist of sand. The rest are stony deserts, where the sand has been blown away, leaving a continuous surface of broken stone; and rock, where the raw rock is often sculpted into strange tower- and mushroom-like shapes called buttes, pedestals and mesas. These shapes are caused by erosion from the sand-carrying wind. Because of the weight of the sand, the wind can only lift it a few metres off the ground. Therefore, the top of the outcrop of harder rock remains almost untouched while the stem will become thinner and thinner until eventually it will be completely worn away.

Desert in the rain

All these areas are arid and bare, devoid of vegetation for the majority of the year, until the rains come. When it does, it comes in torrents. The dry gullies called wadis suddenly fill with water in flash floods. The desert flora takes this chance to bloom and the whole scene comes briefly to life. But after a few days the wet season ends, and the desert returns to aridity. Desolation reigns until the next rainfall allows the plants to grow again.

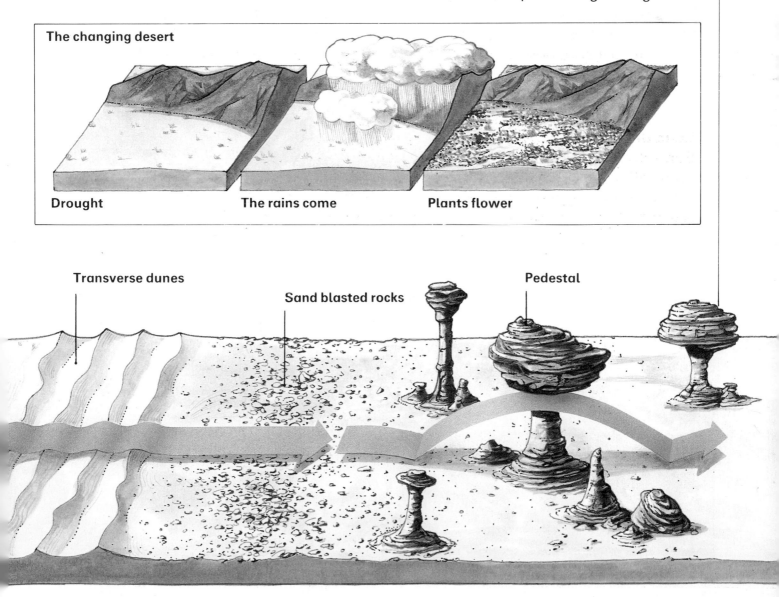

The changing desert

Drought   The rains come   Plants flower

Transverse dunes   Sand blasted rocks   Pedestal

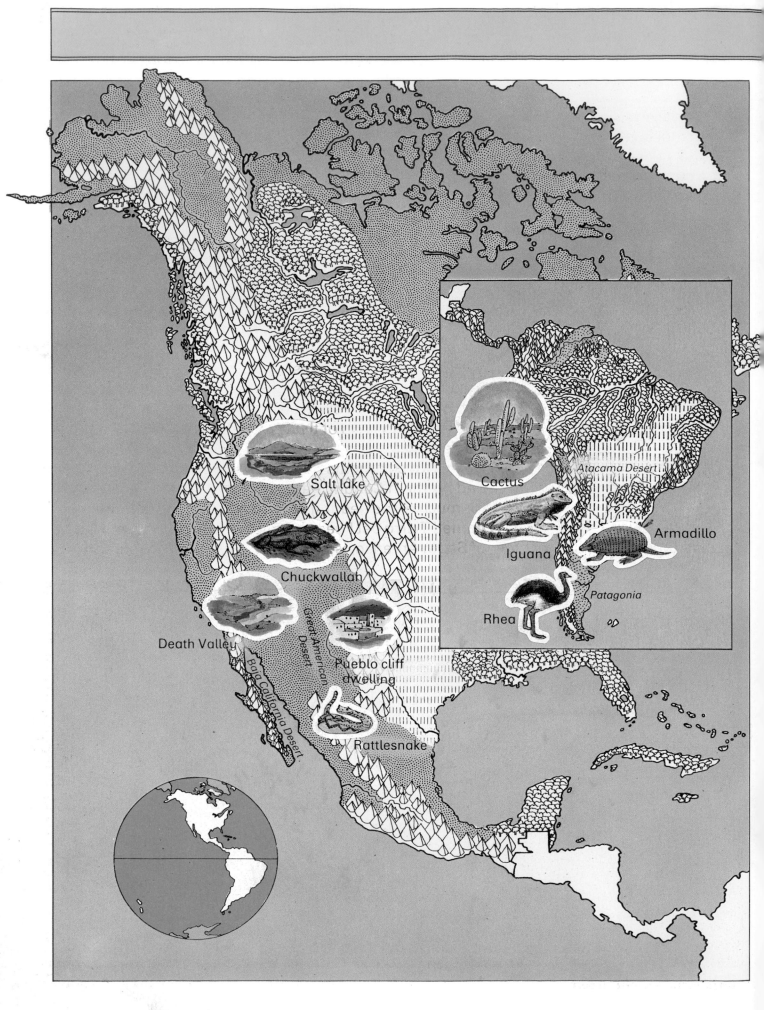

Salt lake

Cactus

Chuckwallah

Atacama Desert

Iguana

Armadillo

Death Valley

Pueblo cliff
dwelling

Rhea

Patagonia

Great American Desert

Baja California Desert

Rattlesnake

North and South America

The Americas, stretching from the scatter of islands near the North Pole, southwards to the bleak tip of Tierra del Fuego, have their share of all the vegetational zones and climatic zones of the world.

The hot desert areas of North America are lumped together as the Great American Desert, covering the western part of the US and the northernmost section of Mexico. Here we have the interior continental desert of the Great Basin, the rain shadow desert of the Mojave and the coastal desert of Baja California.

5500km (3400 miles) away, to the south of the Equator, the southern desert belt begins with the Atacama, along the narrow coastal plain of Peru and Chile. Further inland, in Bolivia, a narrow rain-shadow desert 800km (500 miles) long and 130km (80 miles) wide lies in the Andes mountain range. Further south where the continent begins to taper out, much of the eastern part is rain shadow, sheltered from the wet winds of the Pacific Ocean by the great range of the Andes

The two continents have their cold deserts as well. Alaska and northern Canada lie in the cold tundra zone, covered for much of the year by snow, and the inappropriately named Tierra del Fuego – Land of Fire – at the remotest tip of South America, is held in the grip of a year-round chill.

Deserts and Wastelands

Cacti in the Arizona desert

In the baking heat of the Great American Desert lies Death Valley. Parts of it lie 86m (282ft) below sea level and it is the hottest place on Earth, with temperatures reaching 56.5°C (134°F). Yet, even here, plants and animals manage to survive, for torrents of water fall twice annually.

Moisture for plants

But, so, like anything else living in a desert, the main problem for plants is still finding enough water. This can be achieved in two ways. Some plants, like the creosote bush, are quite small but send out their root system through a vast volume of soil, gathering up every drop of water that is available. This is often done so efficiently that nothing else will grow within several metres of the plant.

The other method is to gather up as much water as possible during the widely-spaced rainy periods, and to store this water and use it through the dry times. The cactus plants of the North American deserts do this. In some of them, such as the giant saguaro cactus, 80 per cent of their weight is water.

These plants protect their supply with waterproof skins to cut down evaporation, and spines to keep away thirsty animals. The desert holly cuts down its evaporation in another way. Its leaves grow almost vertically, so that they catch the light in the morning and evening but are edge on to the searing noon-day Sun.

The desert holly's trick of using only the morning and the evening light is one that has been mastered by most of the desert animals. The dehydrating heat of the full

Saguaro cactus, swollen with water

Poisonous gila monster

White-sided jackrabbit

noon-day desert Sun would be absolutely lethal to any desert-living creature without special adaptations.

Reptiles, such as the cactus-eating chuckwalla lizard and the poisonous gila monster, also conserve their body moisture by being active mostly during the early morning and sheltering during the heat of the day. Most of the rattle-snakes are active both by day and night.

Other methods

The small mammals of the desert remain in their burrows during the day. The air in these burrows is much more humid than the air outside – containing up to five times more moisture than the normal desert air. A sleeping animal breathing this air can retain its body moisture. The kangaroo rat is typical in that its only water comes from the dry plants that it eats. Its body is extremely efficient in converting this unpromising food into water, and it wastes very little in the form of urine – the urine being four times as concentrated as that of other animals.

In moist climates a mammal can cool itself by sweating, but this uses up a lot of moisture. The small desert mammals do not sweat – their small body size means that they have a fairly large skin area compared with their mass, and excess heat can get to the surface quite easily. Larger animals like the kit fox and the jackrabbit have big ears, which give the animal an increased area of skin and act as radiators, again cutting down their need to sweat.

The flesh of the plant-eating animals is the sole source of water for most predators. Flesh-eating animals such as bobcats and horned owls do not need to drink. But birds are not very common in desert areas. Their flying way of life and their wing area make it very difficult to cut down on water evaporation.

Rattlesnake

The Atacama Desert in South America has the lowest rainfall in the world, with 25mm (1in) per year. Moisture reaches the desert mostly by way of fog. Water, evaporated from the Pacific Ocean, condenses in the mountains at a height of about 600m (2000ft) where it creates a belt of foggy forest. This, in turn, gives rise to streams that tumble off the mountains and return the water to the ocean across the desert.

Most desert animals and plants are concentrated along these streams. Only a few cactus and mesquite plants survive away from the water, and a number of geckos and iguana lizards live in the sand. Geckos are of the lizard family and are found in many areas of the world. They can vary from area to area, the structure of their feet, size, and the shape of their tails – the gecko of South America, for example, has a swollen turnip-shaped tail. Larger animals that live in the slightly lusher parts include the rare guanaco.

Desert birds

Two birds of these areas are the ovenbird and the cactus wren. Ovenbirds get their unusual name from their oven-shaped nests. The nests are made of clay, strengthened with grass, with walls up to 40mm (1.5in) thick. The ovenbird builds its nest in winter when the rains make the clay soft enough to work. The birds build new nests every year, the abandoned nests are taken over by hornets, wasps and other birds such as cowbirds.

The rain shadow desert of Patagonia is less bleak than those further north, with scattered tufts of prairie grass. Rodents such as the viscacha and mara also live in these areas.

Patagonian gecko

Ovenbird on its nest

Guanaco in desert scrub

The oldest people of the Great American Desert are the Pueblo of Arizona and New Mexico. The word is Spanish and means a town. It was applied by the Spanish settlers to a number of tribes – mostly the Hopi – who built complicated box-like houses of stone and mud bricks. These structures are sometimes built beneath the overhang of a cliff, and the way in is often a hole in the roof reached by a ladder. They practice what is known as "floodwater farming" in which crops such as maize, gourds and beans are planted in soil irrigated by floods in the rainy season.

Another important people, in fact the largest Indian tribe still existing in North America, are the Navajo, numbering 100,000. They are famous for their weaving and silverware, but most of their skills and traditions they picked up from the Pueblo and the Spaniards.

Desert harvest

Irrigation has been used since before the Spanish conquest to try to produce crops on the excessively dry Atacama Desert of South America. Nowadays, ambitious schemes are in hand to tunnel the vast water supplies from the Amazon basin at the other side of the Andes to the dry western side where it is needed. The crops grown in the irrigated land include rice, sugar cane and cotton.

There are now no native peoples in the arid lands of Patagonia to the south. But well before the Spanish conquest, the Diaguitan Indians had developed irrigation systems using the meltwater from the Andean snows. With the coming of the Europeans, more scientific agricultural schemes were introduced. Nowadays the main crops are cereals, and there is extensive cattle grazing.

Pueblo dwellings, New Mexico

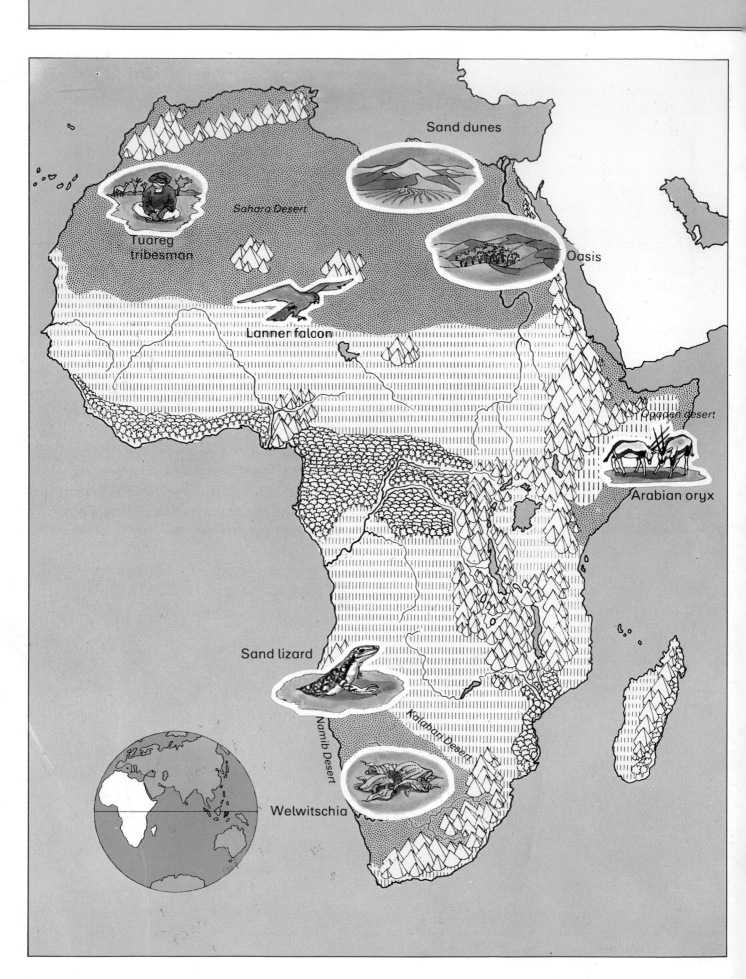

Sand dunes

Sahara Desert

Tuareg
tribesman

Oasis

Lanner falcon

Ogaden desert

Arabian oryx

Sand lizard

Namib Desert

Kalahari Desert

Welwitschia

Africa

The great continent of Africa straddles the Equator, and stretches north and south into the desert climate belts. The northerly desert belt of the continent is very broad, stretching 5500km (3400 miles) from coast to coast, while south of the Equator is much narrower – 2500km (1500 miles) – and tapers off towards the Cape of Good Hope.

The Sahara desert lies in the north, 9,000,000 sq km (3,500,000 sq miles) of it, stretching across the breadth of the continent. It is the largest desert in the world, a vast waterless waste of rock and sand. But the shifting sand dune seas that we normally think of as desert, cover only about a tenth of the Sahara's area. The rest consists of stone, either as stark rugged outcrops and broken plateaux of ancient rock, or as desolate expanses of gravel.

The Namib and Kalahari deserts in the south are smaller but no more hospitable than the great Sahara to the north. The Namib is a sandy coastal strip about 100km (62 miles) wide. The sand dunes here shift northwards constantly, swept along by winds from the south. At the River Kuiseb they suddenly stop, as the sand that tries to spread further is washed away to the sea by the current. The Kalahari reaches eastwards into the interior of the southern part of the continent, a parched upland, but with some desert-type vegetation. Finally, on the eastern Horn of Africa, lie the semi-arid wastes of the Ogaden.

Deserts and Wastelands

Sand desert, Sahara

The many types of lizard living in the Sahara, including the geckos and the skinks, emerge from their burrows in the early morning and present their bodies to the Sun to warm themselves after the chill night. They are most active, and do all their hunting at this time once their blood has warmed up. Reptiles are cold-blooded, that is their body temperature is the same as that of their surroundings, and so they spend much of their time moving from place to place to find a suitable temperature.

Mammals and birds are warm-blooded. They can control their own body heat. But temperatures are so extreme that mammals are forced to behave rather like reptiles. Small mammals sit out the searing day underground and in the evening, when the heat has lessened, they come up to forage and hunt for food in the cool night air.

The common enemy

The creatures that hunt these small mammals also have their adaptations to protect them from the Sun's heat. The fennec, the world's smallest fox, has enormous ears that act as radiators to channel away excess heat from the body. In this way it closely resembles the kit fox of North America.

The lanner falcon is the most abundant bird of prey of the African deserts. Unlike other hawks it tends to glide, supported on the upcurrents of hot air. It can therefore keep its activity to a minimum and hence keep its temperature down. Pairs of lanner falcons often work together, the female disturbing the prey by flying over it, and the male catching it as it breaks cover.

Terebrionid beetle, Namibia

Fennec fox

Lanner falcon

In the south

At the other end of the continent the inhabitants of the scorching Namib desert gain their livelihood from two sources. Prevailing winds from the east bring fine fragments of plant material, and the almost daily fogs bring moisture from the sea. Terebrionid beetles of this area absorb moisture straight from the damp atmosphere. They are preyed upon by the Namibian sand lizard. This cools its body by lifting its feet alternately from the hot sand in a very comical manner.

Some animals, such as Grant's golden mole, have adapted to a life spent *in* the sand. The golden mole has no eyes or external ears. It "swims" through the sand, detecting its prey – insects and small lizards – through the vibrations they make.

A plant unique to this area is the welwitschia, with its huge tattered leaves. Some are many hundreds of years old.

The native peoples of the Sahara consist of three main groups – the Tuareg, who are the most numerous, the Arabs, descended from those who migrated from the Middle East during the seventh and eleventh centuries, and the Negroes, who originated in the Sudan area in East Africa.

The Tuareg, in their uniform blue and white robes, have always existed as nomads, herding sheep, camels and goats. Salt is an important commodity, and the Tuareg run salt caravans from the Niger and Mali to the main livestock areas where it is used in the feed of domestic animals, such as cattle.

Fierce Danakil tribes occupy the Ogaden, and at the other end of the continent the Bushmen people the Kalahari. The Bushmen have a unique physical adaptation to desert life. Their reserves of fat, instead of being deposited beneath the skin of the whole body area, are concentrated around their buttocks. In this way the excess body heat can escape through the skin easily without having to find its way through insulating layers of fat.

Welwitschia, Namibia

Tuareg camel train, Algeria

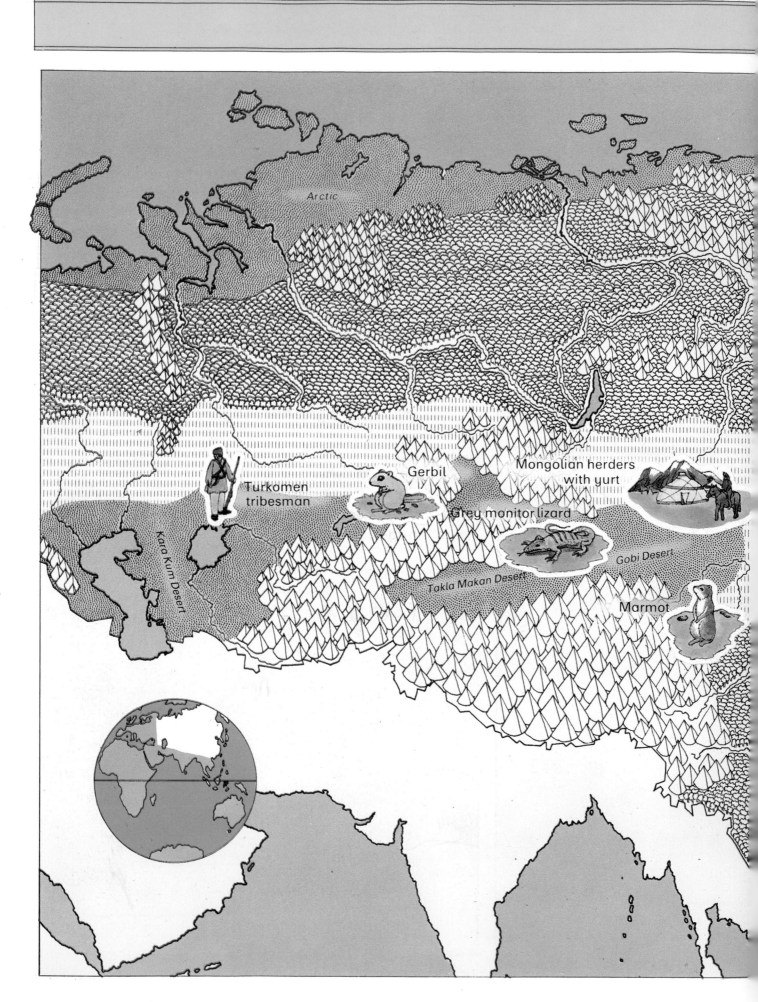

Arctic

Turkomen
tribesman

Gerbil

Mongolian herders
with yurt

Grey monitor lizard

Kara Kum Desert

Takla Makan Desert

Gobi Desert

Marmot

Northern Asia

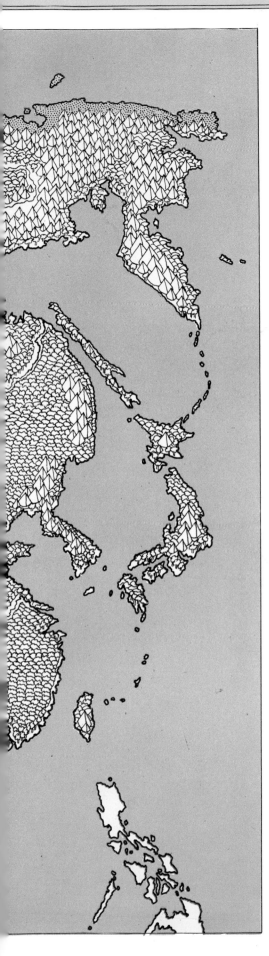

The continent of Asia is so vast that the interior is far from the sea. What little rain there is usually falls only in the spring and autumn, and the rest of the year is dry. From the northern foothills of the Himalayas, arid wastes roll northwards, vast stretches of sand, stone and naked clay, until they merge into the grasslands of the steppes. The prevailing wind is a cold, dry one, blasting down from the Himalayas, and in winter cold air sweeps southwards from the Arctic. In the summer the daytime temperatures are very high but in the winter it is bitterly cold.

The Kara Kum desert near the Caspian and Aral seas to the west, and the Takla Makan desert in the centre are mostly sand. Then a great sweep of clay desert rises to the Tien Shan mountains towards the east. Beyond this range, extending into Mongolia and southern China, is the huge, bleak upland of the Gobi desert, stretching kilometre after arid kilometre of rocks, and pebble-filled valleys almost devoid of any plant growth, except for wild onion and scrub wormwood.

Irrigation, of course, as in all deserts, is an enormous problem, but one which is being very slowly overcome. In the Kara Kum, for example, an 800-km (500-mile) canal brings water from the Amu Darya river near the Aral Sea to irrigate huge cotton plantations.

Rocky wastes of the Gobi

The camel is the animal that most people associate with the desert. The camel of the central Asian deserts is the Bactrian camel, and this differs from the Arabian camel by storing its food in two humps rather than one. And as well as having the thick pads on the feet that prevent it from sinking into sand, the long eyelashes and the closeable nostrils to keep out the blown dust – features it shares with its Arabian cousin – the Bactrian camel has a stocky body, less spindly legs and grows a thick winter coat.

Herds of kulan, the Asian wild ass, and of zeren, the Mongolian gazelle, also live in these deserts, but their numbers have been greatly reduced by hunting. These animals are now protected.

Other mammals

The argali, the wild rock sheep, an ancestor of the domestic sheep, is still found here. This is the largest of the wild sheep species and stands 1.3m (52in) high at the shoulder. As a rule, desert animals are smaller than their relatives elsewhere. Like the sand cat, Blandford's fox, and the desert hedgehog, many also tend to be sand coloured to merge in with their background mainly for protection.

The very small mammals are very much like those of the other desert areas of the world. The rodents, such as the gerbils and jerboas, are omnivorous, eating both animal and plant matter. But the paws of the jerboas living on hard surfaces have five toes to give them grip, whereas

Bactrian camels

jerboas living on soft sand have feathery paws to prevent them from sinking. A unique rodent of central Asia is Seveline's mouse. This eats only insects or other invertebrates (although not the deadly scorpion), of which it needs to consume its own body weight every day. Seed-eating animals do well in the desert, since the seeds have to lie all year on the hard surfaces, waiting for the annual rains to fall before they can germinate.

The reptiles

Reptiles are, as usual, well represented in the Asian deserts. The levantine viper, or kufi, is one of the largest growing up to 120cm (47in). The grey monitor lizard is the most northerly monitor species.

Gerbil with young

Viper

The deserts of North Asia stretch for thousands of kilometres. Therefore, it is not very surprising that they contain many different tribes which are loosely termed Mongols or Turkomen, according to the language they speak.

But there is no clear distinction between their lifestyles; whether they live on the grasslands or the desert, they tend to be sheep herding nomads. Many, however, have been persuaded to settle on state-controlled farms. The introduction of hay-making stations from the 1920's onwards has certainly made it much easier to feed their livestock in winter. Large tracts of desert, especially in Uzbekistan are being irrigated, and now support crops of cotton and wheat.

The most controversial irrigation scheme, recently postponed indefinitely, was to divert some of the water from the north-flowing Asian rivers, so that it ran southwards towards the Caspian and Aral seas. This would have provided water for the western part of the Asian desert, but may have produced serious climatic changes in the far north.

Mongol sheep herding

Southern Asia and Australasia

The vast desert of the Arabian peninsula is an eastward extension of the continental desert of the Sahara, separated from it only by the narrow Red Sea. The whole peninsula is tilted gently to the east. Mountains rise abruptly from the narrow coastal plain of the Red Sea, then the land slopes gently away, across the desolate sandy wastes of the Rub'al-Khali – "the empty quarter" – one of the largest sand deserts in the world, covering an area of 650,000 sq km (251,000 sq miles).

To the north-east, across the Persian Gulf, lies the Iranian desert – a hot, rocky plateau that passes northwards into the sandy and stony deserts of central Asia, and eastwards into the Thar desert of India. The whole Indian subcontinent lies in the desert belt of the Earth, and it is only the yearly, predictable rains brought by the monsoon winds from the Indian Ocean that have kept the main part of India fertile and heavily populated.

Away to the south-east, in the southern desert belt of the Earth, lies the island continent of Australia. The interior of the continent is a bewildering mixture of stony, rocky, sandy and clay desert, usually conveniently divided into two – the Simpson and Gibson deserts. The greater part of the continent is arid, bounded by lush tropical forest in the north and temperate woodland in the south-east and south-west, but in most areas the boundaries between true desert and dry grassland are very indistinct.

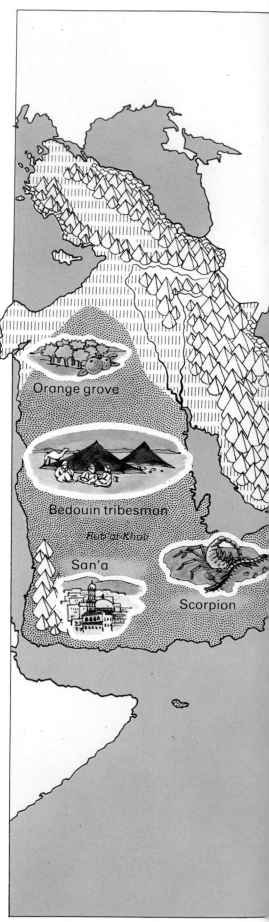

Scrub desert, Northern Territories, Australia

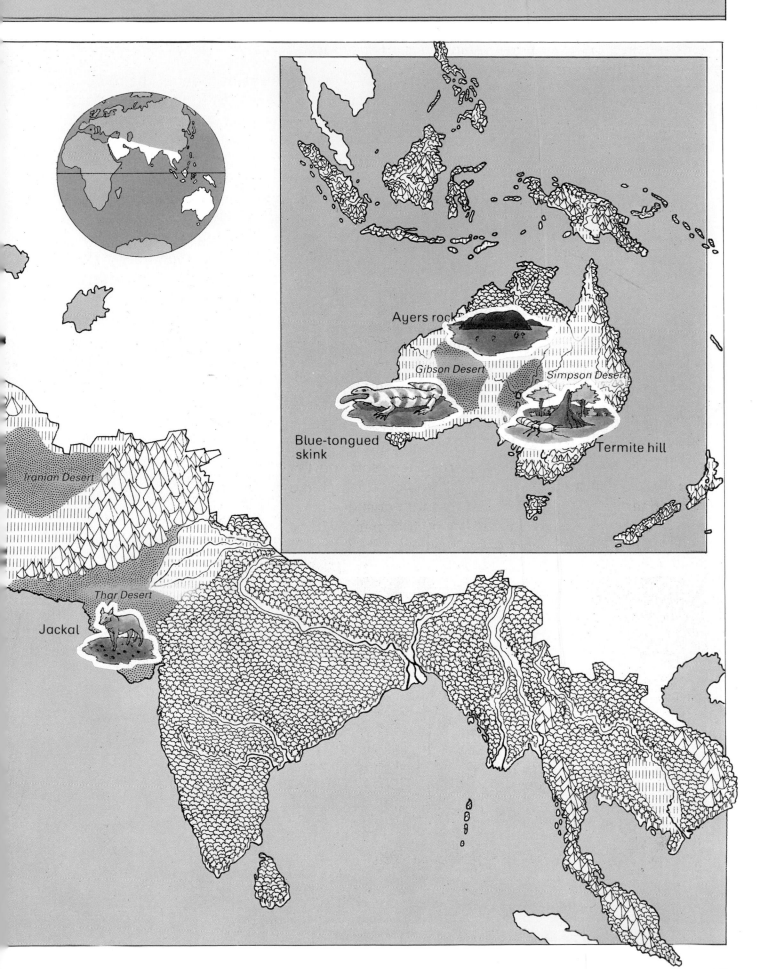

Ayers rock

Gibson Desert

Simpson Desert

Blue-tongued
skink

Termite hill

Iranian Desert

Thar Desert

Jackal

The Rub'al-Khali of the Arabian peninsula does indeed seem to be "the empty quarter" at first glance. The locals call certain sandy wastes "The Anvil of the Sun", so relentless is the heat of the day. Yet even here there is life.

In the deserts of southern Asia most rain falls during the winter, and hence most plants are winter annuals. Because the growing and fruiting season is so short, the seeds that are produced will lie dormant for most of the year, buried in the sand before the following year's rains will germinate them.

Ingenious solutions

The seeds are eaten by insects and by the rodents and the birds of the desert. Such birds include the houbara bustard, a heavy, largely ground-dwelling bird, and the sand grouse, a very distant relative of the grouse of the northern hemisphere.

Unlike the desert rodents, the birds cannot process their food without water, and the birds must stay within reach of water holes to survive. The sand grouse is more imaginative. Not only has it evolved a means of drinking salt water, but it also follows digging animals and waits until theu dig down to moist soil. And the male's method of carrying water back to his fledgelings in his breast feathers is quite unique. Most of the birds of the desert tend to be very drab in colour, in order to camouflage them against their enemies the hawk, desert cat, and snakes.

The Arabian camel thrives on a shrub called camel's thorn. It has a high water content and can be used by the camel to produce fat, which is then stored in the hump. The camel can drink up to 120 litres (30 gallons) at a time and, during particularly harsh periods, can lose up to a quarter of its weight without ill effect.

Arabian oryx

Cobra, Thar desert

Threatened species

The other large mammals of the southern Asian desert are the Arabian gazelle and Arabian oryx. Both have been almost exterminated by hunting. They were the traditional quarry of the local people, the Bedouin, and used to be hunted only in the winter when their horses could survive the open desert. Then, with the coming of trucks and helicopters, hunting could take place all year round and the herds began to decline. As exploration for oil started in the area, they were systematically hunted as a source of food for the oil crews, and this almost succeeded in causing their extinction. The last known wild oryx was shot in 1972. But a few oryx had been kept in captivity in the United States. Some were returned to Oman, and both the oryx and Arabian gazelle are now protected species and their numbers are steadily increasing once more.

Male sand grouse

The Bedouin have swarthy skins and typically long noses – the latter being an adaptation to cool and moisten the air that is breathed. Their religion is Islam and they are world-famous for their hospitality, their honesty and their proud independence.

Like most desert peoples, they are nomadic, relying on scattered oases to water their herds of sheep and goats. A few have settled, creating desert towns such as San'a in the Yemen. Towns and oases are usually surrounded by groves of date palms. Its fruit provides the Bedouin with food and drink. The stones are fed to the camels. The leaves are used as fuel, the fibres to make ropes, and the trunks are used for building. In the shade of the trees can be grown limes, lemons, figs, olives, wheat, maize, beans and peas. The people are often nomadic only during the rainy season. The dry times they spend close to the wells and oases. But successful irrigation schemes have , especially in the Negev desert, transformed once barren wastes into fertile citrus fruit groves and vegetable fields.

Bedouin family

Until quite recently the native people of Australia, the Aborigines, still carried on a hunter-gatherer existence – as did their ancestors who migrated from South East Asia about 30,000 years ago. They lived and travelled throughout the desert in small clans, hunting kangaroos and wallabies with boomerangs and spears, and gathering bulbs and roots, as well as grubs and termites. Aborigines still have complex rituals that accompany every aspect of their lives, and visit sacred sites such as the famous Ayers Rock. The most well-known is the custom of "walkabout" in which a young man will leave the clan and wander, possibly for years in the desert, teaching himself the arts of life and survival.

The Aborigines that wandered in the desert adapted to their environment without the encumbrance of personal possessions. They wore no clothes, the Sun warming them during the day and camp fires at night, and any dwellings were very temporary. These consisted of sticks and grass, acting as a shelter from the wind. Many, however, have now settled down in townships, and find work on ranches.

Aborigines in ceremonial dress

Similar but different

There is a natural phenomenon called "convergent evolution" that means that different animals have evolved the same shapes to fit them to the same lifestyles. Nowhere can this be seen more clearly than in Australia. The island continent has been separated from the other continental masses for 80 million years. During this time the animal life has developed independently from that anywhere else in the world.

But despite being very different, the individual animals have evolved shapes and lifestyles appropriate to their desert surroundings, that are identical to those adopted on the other continents, by the more familiar types of mammal.

Red kangaroo

Examples

Kangaroos are the largest mammals that live here. They are mainly grassland animals but, like camels, they can travel great distances over waterless wastes in search of food and drink. Like desert antelopes, they have evolved a means of removing poisons from their bodies without the use of water, and so they urinate rarely. The quokka is a small wallaby, about the size of a rabbit. It lives on Rottnest Island off the west coast. There is no fresh water at all here, and the quokka can drink salt water without ill effect. Antechinomys is a tiny marsupial that looks exactly like a desert mouse. It bounds across the desert sands, balanced by its long tail, and has the same diet of invertebrates and seeds as all desert rodents all over the world.

The smaller animals are preyed upon by goshawks and peregrine falcons. These birds do not drink water, gaining all the moisture they need from the flesh of their prey. The birds of Australia are not as unique as the mammals, since the oceans are less of a barrier to a creature able to stay aloft over long distances.

Australian reptiles

Reptiles are particularly common in the Australian sands, especially snakes. These, such as the brown snake and the bandy bandy, spend the heat of the day buried in the sand. Many of the lizards are burrowers too, and some have only tiny legs, such as the blue-tongued and stump-tailed skinks, to help them to "swim" in the sand. Desert arthropods are usually either arachnids, such as spiders and scorpions, or insects. The arachnids are mostly predators, lying in ambush for, or actively hunting down, the insects.

In the very driest areas there are thorny acacias called mulga and stunted eucalyptus, called mallee. Spinifex grass grows under less arid conditions and with this the deserts grade into grasslands.

Blue-tongued skink

Scorpion with young

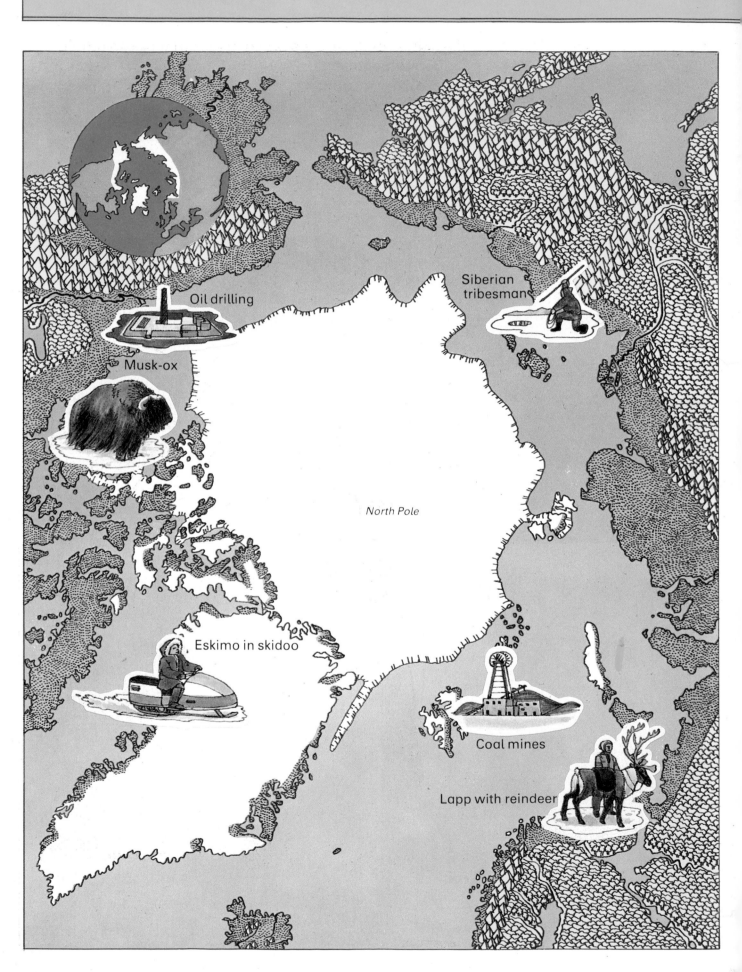

Oil drilling

Siberian tribesman

Musk-ox

North Pole

Eskimo in skidoo

Coal mines

Lapp with reindeer

Arctic and Antarctica

If we think of deserts as being places that are so totally inhospitable that practically nothing will grow or live, the most obvious examples must be the North and South Poles. Here the Sun is so low in the sky that it spreads little warmth on the ground, and for a large part of the year it does not rise at all. The area around the North Pole is all ocean, while that around the South Pole is an actual continental land mass. Both places are covered in thick ice, and with constant piercingly-cold winds, the polar ice caps are the bleakest and most unwelcoming places on Earth.

The Arctic may be a frozen ocean, but it is fringed by proper land, frozen rock ranges rising from the ice. Greenland is the largest of these land masses, although it is really several large islands covered by a single ice sheet. Others, such as Iceland, and the northern archipelago of Spitzbergen, have their shores bathed by the relatively warm water brought up from the tropics by the current called the North Atlantic Drift.

Antarctica, the ice-covered continent, is the coldest place on Earth. A temperature of −88°C (−126°F) has been recorded there. Along the coast the ocean keeps the temperature fairly moderate and brings fresh snow and even rain, but inland it is arid and swept by dry winds. Here fresh snow very rarely falls.

Desert regions

Ice

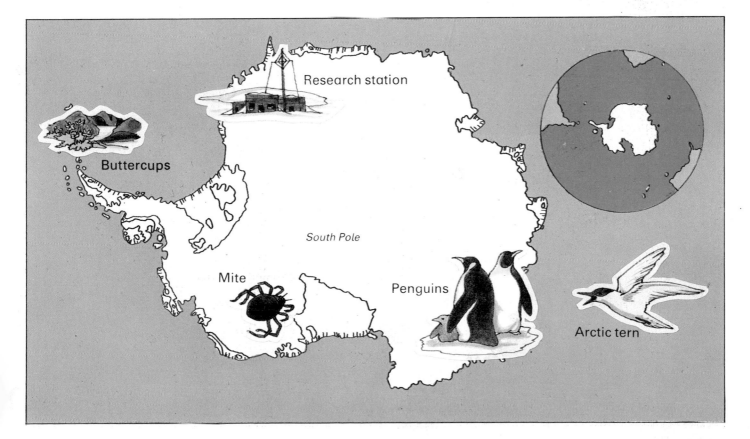

Research station

Buttercups

South Pole

Mite

Penguins

Arctic tern

The ice of Antarctica is 4.5km (2.8 miles) thick in places and represents 90 per cent of the Earth's fresh water. However, there are a number of places that are free of it — mostly coastal strips and upland valleys — but these only amount to about 4 per cent of the land area. Life does exist on these chill naked rocks, but it is sparse. The coldest driest places have only lichen, clinging in thin encrustations to the exposed rocks, while mosses struggle to survive in damper, more sheltered corners.

Low bushes of flowering plants grow on the continent only on the Antarctic Peninsula, where it reaches northwards towards South America. Some of the sub-antarctic islands, such as South Georgia, support meadows of low alpine flowers such as buttercups during the short spring and summer months.

Cold comfort

Amongst the naked rocks and thin lichens of the ice-free areas, there is very little animal life. Tiny worms, mites and a bird known as the springtail are almost the only creatures, and these only survive because their body fluids contain a kind of natural antifreeze.

Along the edge of the pack-ice the penguins live. These roost on the ice and feed on ocean fish. They are, in turn, preyed on by seals and skuas. Elephant seals and fur seals are common on many of the islands throughout the Antarctic waters, and the albatross wheels in the cold skies. Another bird that is common in the Antarctic summer is the Arctic tern.

The Arctic wastes seem to be more hospitable to life than their southern counterparts. This is largely due to the fact that the warm North Atlantic Drift brings

Reindeer grazing on the tundra

warmer water to many of the lands bordering the Arctic ice cap. Tundra vegetation can grow in the Arctic islands and some sparse forests even occur on the coastal areas of Iceland.

Larger animals

Musk-oxen used to be very common, ranging over most of the northern hemisphere during the Ice Age. Since then they have become quite rare, being hunted almost to extinction in the islands of the Canadian Arctic and on Greenland, their last natural homes. Now, however, colonies have been established artificially in Spitzbergen and their numbers are increasing once more.

Further south the largest herbivore is the reindeer. This comes north to the edge of the tundra in the summer and migrates south to the coniferous forests for the winter. One predator of this region and the greatest threat to both reindeer and musk-ox is the wolf.

The people of the far north depend for their livelihood on the sea. The Eskimo, or Innuit of Canada and Alaska are fisher folk and seal hunters. The area is, however, very rich in oil.

Greenland was settled by Viking farmers in the tenth century, but this was during a phase when the climates were less harsh than at present. There is no farming there now but a modern fishing industry sustains the population. Spitzbergen has coal mines, worked by Norway and the Soviet Union.

In northernmost Europe the Lapps depend on the reindeer. They follow the herds as they migrate northwards from their winter forests to a place half way along the route where the calves are born. Then they follow them to the tundra for the summer grazing and follow them back to the forest for the winter. The Tungus, and especially the Chukchi tribes of Siberia live in much the same way.

There are no native people on Antarctica, only a number of research stations involved in scientific studies.

Musk-ox, Greenland

Research station in Antarctica

The Future of the Environment

All the other environments of the world – the tropical forests, the temperate grasslands, the temperate woodlands – are shrinking as time goes on. Only the deserts are growing.

The southern boundary of the Sahara desert is advancing at a rate of about 100m (330ft) per year. On the edges of the Thar desert in Pakistan and India are barren areas which were, within living memory, fertile farmlands. In a longer term view, the Tassili plateau in the centre of the Sahara has rock paintings executed some 5000 years ago. These show giraffes, elephants, rhinoceros and herds of antelope, stalked by lions – all animals that could not possibly exist in these desolate areas nowadays. When they were painted, the surrounding landscape must have been grasslands with scattered stands, or copses, of trees.

To emphasize this, not far from the paintings grow some ancient trees – gnarled cypresses with tap roots 30m (98ft) long to soak up the little water available. But trees like these could not possibly germinate under the conditions found there now. They started growing 2000 or 3000 years ago, when the climate and the landscape were moister. What has happened to change it?

Reasons for change

About 10,000 years ago the Ice Age ended. When that happened the belts of rain that had covered most of northern Africa retreated northwards and the Sahara area dried out. Another, significant reason is again to be found in the Tassili paintings. Here we see men herding cattle away.

Under very dry conditions a natural flora and fauna has developed over the centuries, adapted to that environment. However, if the delicate balance of the right number of animals eating the right number of plants is upset, then the whole fragile system may collapse. This upset can be caused by overgrazing.

Dry lakebed, Australia

Not only do domesticated herds strip the greenery from the ground, they also trample the soil into a solid cake. The little rain that does fall cannot soak into the packed soil, and with no vegetation cover to keep it in place the water evaporates straight away, or runs off very quickly to cause destructive and wasteful flash floods in the wadis.

Dead plant material adds richness to the soil, and grass roots hold the soil together. Once the grasses have been grazed away, the soil is lifted by the wind and blown about as a fine dust and is eventually lost.

A temporary desert

This is not just theory, it has been seen in practice. Northern Uganda in Africa, was rapidly becoming a new desert, due to overgrazing by domestic cattle. Then the area became infested by deadly tsetse flies that attacked the cattle, and so the cattle herders moved on. Vegetation has now returned to this abandoned area.

Irrigation

If human population is going to continue to increase, the advance of the deserts must be halted, and the marginal areas must be made fertile again. This, however, is going to be a long and very complicated process.

The most obvious way of doing this is to bring in water from somewhere. In parts of the Sahara, the Great American desert, and the Negev desert in the Near East, water is being brought up from moist rocks deep underground. However, these rocks were soaked during the Ice Age, and the water will not last forever.

Most irrigation techniques rely on the provision of large areas of water brought, possibly, from nearby mountains. Most of this water then evaporates in the heat before it can do any good. The storage lakes and reservoirs also provide ideal breeding grounds for organisms that produce devastating human diseases, such as malaria and bilharzia.

Irrigated fields of Akhdar, Oman

Interesting facts

The camel can lose as much as 30 per cent of its body weight because of dehydration. At this stage the camel can drink up to 104 litres (23 gallons) at one time without harming itself. The camel has red blood cells that are egg-shaped and therefore are able to expand quickly into spheres to absorb the sudden intake of water.

Snakes, such as the diamondbacked rattlesnake found in the deserts of North America, can swallow whole, live prey. This is because their upper jaws are attached only loosely to the skull, and the lower jaw is split into two halves joined by elastic ligaments, so they can be moved separately as the prey is forced down the snake's throat.

Even desert snakes cannot survive in the harsh daytime temperatures of the desert. Scientists experimented by placing a snake in direct sunlight. It immediately started writhing. Five minutes later the writhing stopped and after seven minutes all bodily movement stopped. The snake was dead within ten minutes.

The greatest temperature drop between midday and midnight was recorded in the Sahara desert. It dropped from 52°C (126°F) to −2°C (26°F).

Carp have recently been discovered living in poisonous sulphur lakes in the middle of the Sahara desert. Freshwater fish have also been found in deep underground streams.

Shrimps can also be found in deserts. When the infrequent rains come, drought-resistant eggs of shrimp-like crustaceans that have lain dormant since previous rains, which may have been as much as 25 years before, come to life. They must mature and lay eggs before the pools dry up again, so their active life span often lasts no longer than two weeks.

Sometimes moisture in the Sahara produces a phenomenon called *fech-fech*. Damp air sticks the sand grains together on the desert surface, forming a rigid crust. Wheeled vehicles can break through this crust and become bogged down in the soft sand beneath.

A single tree – L'Arbre du Ténéré – is marked on local maps and used as a landmark in the Sahara in the centre of Niger. There is no other tree for about 50km (30 miles), yet in 1960 a lorry driver crashed into it!

Rocks showing fossilized sand dunes indicate that great areas of the Earth now in temperate regions, were covered in desert 350 million and 250 million years ago.

Great wealth is often found in deserts. The Namib has diamonds, the Atacama has phosphates and nitrates, the Great Basin has gold and the Simpson has nickel. The nitrates of the Atacama are now no longer mined as extensively as they once were since the chemical has been replaced by modern synthetic fertilizers.

Shrimps hatched in puddles, Sahara

Glossary

Scientists use many special words to describe deserts and wastelands and the wildlife found in deserts and wastelands. These are some of the most common ones you are likely to come across.

Aborigines   The native people of Australia.

Alluvial   Deposited by flowing water, as in a river or stream.

Archipelago   A group of islands, usually in a line.

Arthropod   A zoological term that means animals with jointed feet, wings or legs, such as insects and spiders.

Bedouin   The native desert people of the Middle East and north Africa.

Blizzard   A wind storm driving snow before it.

Coastal desert   A desert produced by dry air descending over a cold sea current near a coast.

Desert   Any area that has less than 30cm (12in) of rain per year.

Equator   The imaginary line that runs right round the Earth mid way between the North and South poles.

Flash flood   A sudden torrent of water produced in a watercourse that is usually dry, by heavy rainstorms.

Fledgeling   A young bird.

Germinate   The process where a plant sprouts, buds, or develops new shoots.

Interior continental desert   A desert found in the middle of a continent, so far from the sea that no moist winds reach it.

Irrigation   The supply of water (usually artificially) to an otherwise dry area.

Lichen   A primitive plant consisting of cells of algae combined with cells of a fungus. It is often found encrusting rocks or growing in tufts.

Marsupial   One of a large group of mammals found almost exclusively in Australia, in which the immature young are carried about in a pouch – as opposed to the placental mammals of the rest of the world that give birth to well-advanced young.

Nomad   People who spend their lives moving from place to place, usually following herds of animals on their migration routes.

Outback   An Australian term for the wild interior of the continent.

Peninsula   A piece of land surrounded on three sides by water and joined at the fourth to a larger land mass.

Permafrost   A layer of frozen soil in Arctic or Antarctic areas that remains frozen all year round.

Pingo   A rounded hill pushed up by the action of freezing water.

Predator   An animal that lives by hunting and eating other animals.

Rain shadow desert   A desert produced on the lee side of a mountain range. Any moisture in the wind will have been dropped on the windward side on its passage over the range.

Steppes   The grasslands of central Asia.

Tropic   One of two imaginary lines on the Earth, 23½°N and 23½°S, marking the limits of the area in which the Sun is overhead at some time of the year.

Tuareg   The native people of the Sahara desert.

Tundra   The landscape near the North Pole where no trees grow, but is not covered by snow for the whole year.

Wadi   A dry desert stream bed that usually only fills after a desert downpour.

Weathering   The process by which a rock breaks down through the influence of rain, wind and other climatic factors.

Yurt   A tent of skins or felt pulled over poles, as used in central Asia.